THE PAST IS NEVER DEAD

HANS VAN DE WAARSENBURG

THE PAST IS NEVER DEAD

SELECTED POEMS

Translated by Peter Boreas

 **EYEWEAR** PUBLISHING

First published in 2013
by Eyewear Publishing Ltd
74 Leith Mansions, Grantully Road
London w9 1lj
United Kingdom

Typeset with graphic design by Edwin Smet
Author photograph Harry Heuts
Printed in England by TJ International Ltd, Padstow, Cornwall

All rights reserved
© 2013 Hans van de Waarsenburg
© 2013 Peter Boreas *Translations*

The right of Hans van de Waarsenburg to be identified as author of this work has been asserted in accordance with section 77 of the Copyright, Designs and Patents Act 1988
ISBN 978-1-908998-09-5

WWW.EYEWEARPUBLISHING.COM

Hans van de Waarsenburg
is a respected Dutch literary figure.
He was born in Helmond, Netherlands in 1943 and
published his first collection of poems, entitled
Gedichten (*Poems*), in 1965. His collection *De
vergrijzing* (*The Greying*) was awarded the prestigious
Jan Campert Prize for Poetry in 1973. In March 2004
he received the first Municipal Award of the Helmond
Town Council for his life's work. Between 1997 and
2000 he was chairman of the PEN Centre
of the Netherlands. From 1997-2012 he was
chairman of The Maastricht International
Poetry Nights, a biannual international
poetry festival.

Peter Boreas (b.1945) studied
English language and literature. For thirty-odd
years he taught English at secondary schools in the
Netherlands, but now works as a freelance translator
in the village of Banholt. His translations, which include
work by Ilya Kaminsky, Amir Or and a number of
Dutch poets, have been published by The Maastricht
International Poetry Nights, Verlag Ralph Liebe, Azul
Press and the Bonnefant Press.

Table of Contents

SEASCAPES 1981

In two-sided light — 12
The stillness of ashes — 13
A butterfly of reflection — 14
The negative of time — 15
Small song — 16
Diptych — 17
Wet washcloth in daylight — 18
Looking glass letter — 19
I do not lie down — 20
I am writing you — 21
Tide — 22
Thoughts, placed on — 23
Sea stone — 24
Saw the land — 25
Stone that embellishes rivers — 26
Catafalque — 27
Rope — 28
Dune house — 29
The sea, the journeys — 30
Final change — 31

ALAS, TIME 1985

Picture postcard — 32

WHERE THE BLUE ENDS 1987

The boathouse at Laugharne — 33
Where the blue ends — 34
Movement — 35
Firmament — 35
Horizon — 36
Cloth — 36
Tranparant — 37
Fisherman — 37
Windjammer — 38
The sails — 38
The painter visits the beach — 39

THE THIRST OF PORTS 1990

Lisbon — 40
Bahia Blanca — 41
Asparagus, asparagus
  (Felled by lust) — 42
Remember: the civilized patter,
  the steaming — 42
These frigid fingers of darkloving
  death — 43
The land of dawn is in the earth — 44
What makes it so translucent,
  so palatable — 45
No fast and loose in this: bleached — 46
After the days of pricks and parties — 47
Early Harbour — 48
Prayer for silent islands — 49

EVENING FALL 1993

Paricutin — 50
The view slowly discolouring — 50
The coastline shifts — 51
Terra salsa — 52
Lo there appeared — 52
He slid into the breakers — 53
For ever the step — 54
Ripple — 55
Because everything — 56
He stands in a distant country and pulls the flaking blue — 56
Because everything perishes, he deceives the night with — 56
Because everything perishes, only the precious remains in — 56
Blue agave — 57
Farewell — 58
Sitting at the table — 59
Sitting at the table, you — 59
The years do not change — 60
In memoriam Lei Molin — 61

SOUTH WALL 1995

South Wall — 62
Brewhouse Farm — 64
Divine spud — 66
Was it on the IJzer or the Scheldt — 66
Which he dried and sprinkled with salt in a — 67
Weekly caused by Catholic fish — 68
Divine spud II — 69
They ate you since — 69
You were a prole between — 70
You grew in armpits of clay — 71
Well, sand groveller, I always — 72
I meet you everywhere in a plurality — 73
Nehalennia — 74
The rushing of waves in the night — 74
She waded in luminous foam — 75
In December, when time stands still — 76
Only at springtide you still — 77
Trees — 78
Since all must pass — 79
Adíos pampa mío — 80
Milonga — 81
Walker — 82
While he walks – He walks — 83
Mondrian in Domburg — 84
Sierra Bermeja — 85
Misanthrope — 86
Don Quixote in landscape — 87
Itamaracá *The song of Fort Orange* — 88
Cape Death — 89

DESCRIBING THE LAKE 2000

Descriptions of the lake — 90
Islands — 98
Evening light (*Maastricht*) — 101
Maas /Meuse — 103
Leaf, leaves — 105
Across the fields — 106
Galway — 107
Aran Islands — 108
*The ferry to the islands cleft
   the waves* — 108
Sailor's legs felt for the quay — 109
*Shivering we covered ourselves
   in blankets* — 110

WHEREVER THE ROADS WENT 2003

On the death of a
   Colorado · 580 kg — 111
The playing field seemed open — 111
Stubborn anger weeps — 112
Nostalgia for those green days — 113
The Rock 'n' Roll Poems — 114
The days before Rock 'n' Roll
Just you try — 114
Johnny Weissmuller — 115
Bill Haley in Maastricht — 116
What had not assailed the ears — 116
Time languishes in vinyl — 117
The last Waltz — 118

Yonder, to Ghent — 120
There was nothing yet — 120
But Ghent was his life — 121
The boy standing there — 122
In the world — 123
In wakeful sleep — 124
My knowledge is supported — 125

Maastricht Pub Crawl — 126
La Vierge — 126
Café 't Haantje — 127
Tribunal — 128
Walker — 129
Wine is a mocker — 130
Studio — 131
Going down slow — 132
Glass — 133

AZUL 2006

Dad — 134
Many years and some months — 134
This is a night to remember — 135
I do not now remember — 136
We have never had — 137
You settled with her — 138
Mother — 139
Slow approach — 140
Altar boy — 141
Dead poet — 142
Azul — 143
Budapest 1956 — 144
Il Castello di Duino — 145
Polskie tango — 146

A LATE VISITOR 2009

For the love of women — 147
There is the sea — 147
There is the sea and you're back — 148
There is the sea, where he smirks — 149
For poet and painter
    Paul Snoek — 150
No, I won't forget you — 150
Raise a jug of water — 151
Your soul was in your eyes — 152
Raise your head — 153
Nocturnes — 154
Do the tones — 154
Glass beads yes — 155
How do fingers — 156
I hide in the crook — 157
How to forget — 158
A farewell — 159
The mother is chiselled — 160
How wind can blow — 161
Come, let us travel — 162
Hesitant words — 163

The Unending Song /
    Canto Ostinato — 164
The poet, squatting down — 164
Through Zeeland — 165
I am always wanting — 166
Marram in the dunes of brine — 167
Reduced hearing — 168
Crystal sparkle — 169
Lifeless sails — 170

It is one of those nights — 171
When tractors — 171
When my father sits — 172
That envelop me — 173

SHADOW EDGE 2012

Consul — 174
Bathing in sweat — 174
Lovingly he fills — 175
Thus he wakes — 176
The Consul writes — 177
I will call her — 178

Notes — 180

**The past is never dead.
It's not even past.**

William Faulkner

In two-sided light

The sea at the level of the land,
the house disturbs the roofs.
Winged words beat down
in wind and foam,
only death can still reach him.

He flattens dune-grass, damp
dune-sand rises up.
Gulls brush foam and wind
into his dark recesses.

There a father rises,
who cries out in pain with pain.
The sun still lies on the dune,
the sea has been singing too long through his house.

Slowly he stumbles past the clouds,
the rising tide draws him from the beach.

In two-sided light our hands reach out.

The stillness of ashes

In the open wounds of blossom and
fresh green, the seal calls him.
He sees the water
grow hard as clear glass.

A limping melancholy rainstorm
bobbing on barren ground
no longer saves anything.
The doors banged closed.

Wind rustles overhead.
The vacuum expands.
A dream of warmth and sorrow
shatters against clear glass.

Shrivels and withers to the stillness of ashes.

A butterfly of reflection

While walking through the lanes,
the sea foam of time.

The daily mumblings
that take to the street.
The sun taut on the face.

Firemen are sliding
from eye to eye:

A butterfly of reflection.
A bird in the beak.

The coastline cuts it open,
the tide buries the image.

He becomes his own hands,
the sweat that plays in them.

The negative of time

In this hard land soft stone of seasons,
where autumn is no longer accidental.
The white linen cloth seems to have
been lowered permanently on the face,

mirrors out of the shadow
grow daily colder.
Until she takes her place:

making visible
what has been written,
rubs herself into him with soft lips.

The way you walk through the evening, he says then.
The way you don't give a damn for the day
finishes me.

Awakens the pike in my tongue
and the amoebe of your lips.
Fighting all about me in naked skin against death.

Not keeping a shred of shame,
in this negative of time.

Small song

What you have been runs after you:
each season you change the child

Sometimes this small song sounds
that stretches the day, the smell that recalls it

The mouth that won't gargle with salt
or swallow cod-liver oil or a rusty bike

Also the hunger, which was no hunger
lard and the warmth of your darned sweater,
old newspapers and snow under your wooden shoes

summer meadows green with adventure
and the future once more frozen solid: child that
you dream in silence, without the harness of time

What you have been runs after you
the child that withdrew further and further
from you, that sees you go

And wherever you return to,
each year the snapshots of childhood
are shuffled differently.

Diptych

The old engine of dailyness:
light slipped under the eyelids,
lumbered toward the retina

Past the sea, where dim light still lingers,
he remembered the hesitant steps
that preceded him on his way

Things happened in the head lying
still, the motionless body: the father,
spotless surgeon, the mother covered with jewels

the first steps in the dark, hands
in front of the eyes; night velvet
in the morning when I fled

The first steps taken, finally past
sea-music, the senses; no one has
been able to save this child from the waves.

Wet washcloth in daylight

This is as it should be: you don't look up or back,
shake your mane, and somewhere in a space
you see yourself mirrored: someone looks
at you, shakes his mane:

The Droste cocoa tin, into which you
slip away yourself: diminishing face,
perspective that disappears from itself.
A morning's mirror through which you slip away.

The sea audible as a cracking shell,
teeth of poor alloy, eyes in the
frosted glass of years; the tired
kingdom of the body, what remains:

a voice hastening through the days,
pits in the sound at times, or a
helpless creaking that, in any case
is no longer overheard.

A word that still scratches Altamira
a bison stretching its back.
The chalk, fingered by your hand:
ice age, primeval ox, sea view, stammering mosquito:

Who knows whether death has not
already settled under the skin.
Every dream misplaced and an
accomplice to the intruding enemy.

Looking glass letter

I am writing you a slow mirror letter
a letter of time in which steps were
taken, words said and written:

a letter of time, past, which hardly
still reaches, the way a blind spot deteriorates
into ash in the palm of my hand

into the snipped off edge of a photograph
that grows smaller and smaller.

I do not lie down my head at this, the voice
is still speaking, the fingers bend: behind
the retina the seasons turn back:

the months forgotten, the names erased,
for they grew bitter as faces
in which the wound of birth was never healed

in which time always passing by the head
armours the years. I'm writing you.

I'm writing you a letter of time, winters
while the hours scrape the bottom,
your face, still visible, pushes the garden gate

the shutters of Villa Carmen Sylva,
this house that rests on old aristocracy, dune and wind

where your warm sea voice says: time must be peeled
round this corner.

Tide

Tide which turns inward
towards land

Which, locked out,
opens the eye

which tucks in the storm
with water-soft hands, tide

a book full of sand traces
salt in open wounds

Tide, worn out
to lunatic leaping

erased.

Thoughts, placed on the rising
of water, the washing
of water

The drying of sun
The blowing of wind
Cruel tide of youth

Wears out hair
Sharpens words round and round

Thoughts placed on the
rising water, the
washing water:

Tide,
that lasts and lasts.

Sea stone

Accompanying on travels
in this skin, your membrane of stem
in the creaking brain

Train after train moved the years
each trail a dead end.

Saw the land that
lies within frontiers.

Old land, plundered dry
weeping land full of holes.
Windy reeds, silent

expecting the opposite shore:

a place to hide, a right
a place to be found

a stone polished smooth.

Stone that embellishes rivers
sleeping in their beds
never offering bread
never bent crooked

Sea stone,

image that constantly turns, rolls over
as if mirroring itself:

the head born for the first time,
the folds, the earliest skin blemishes:

Sea stone.

Catafalque

Always the message of water
leans on the bannister of the voice

Seeks a grip on the ears
of a shifted century

Laughable the dried seaweed
on a head of seafoam

Carrying all findings to
the floodline, laughable

This catafalque of primal sorrow
this open wound scraped by tide after tide:

What you stare at in wind, you wear out in time.

Rope

Rope that unravels
the ship's skin that rusts
the helpless caulking
of hope

The eyes are sun-burned
spots on the iris

This ear has holes
in the wind

All adding up to death.

Dune house

The dune house sorrows through the summer
the hand behind a landspit
a prow of emptiness

The last seaclap that counts
(that counts)

And the light salted
time engraved:

Whoever stores the sea
will always see land.

The sea, the journeys

The sea, the journeys that keep moving on
day after day in your falling shadow

The words, always those images
the eye of the needle
your skin growing shallower

The voice also, which you do not take along
into the creaking brain
the rooms that never figure in the slides

And the evening air, restless, wall to wall:

Always the words
the writing hand that moves.

Final change

The dune stretches its back
and at times he can still speak
can still see

The change
of a tiny tailfin
the slap of the waves

Then he hears the downpour
of rain on the timeless skylight
and a pale song

His hand grows no lighter
in the hush of what
slides by

The hours lead him further
away than ever from what
was desired

He is seated and has
in time become a tributary
of the drab, grey water

Only his eyes still, his mouth
when the sea grows phosphorescent
and remains so.

Picture postcard

Your hand mirrors the map
This shadow of your travelling:

With the harbour the land disappears,
Before the wind out of the foam

Then the figurehead,
Inaudible the breakers

The horizon looks like a home
A hallucination for seamen
And what remained hidden:

The glass that you knocked over,
The ink that ran,

The words that were washed.

The boathouse at Laugharne

We're having tea and write picture postcards
Light of forgetfulness hangs over the Irish Sea
Beyond this the ocean treading water
Stanzas in a posthumous tourist life

Thirty-nine, thirty-nine. A few more months to go
Ambiguous in death or one's birthday
Saving up thirst like ebb, until the tide washed
The boathouse, the wind returned with sluggish motion

You sat down, I stood about. How much longer
This going places together, out of time
This never-ending dream of ships departing
An emigrant going down in blotchy corn

From the platform we watched the same view
Low tide that afternoon, discolouring the mud
You in his chair, tearing up time (a card?):
'Do not go gentle into that good night'

Crumbs, cake and china, and milkwood
In our tea. I do not dare to check this light
There is a hole in time and the nagging
Of a hangover. Darkness reflected, it is getting later.

WHERE THE BLUE ENDS

Doch die Möwe, aus den Lüften,
Schieszt herunter auf das Fischlein,
Und den raschen Raub im Schnabel,
Schwingt sie sich hinauf ins Blaue.

Heinrich Heine, *Meeresstille*
(*Die Nordsee*, 1825-1826)

Movement

Rest
for
the sails

Till the
lull in the wind
falters

Movement
slowly
arises

The knife
is whetted

To wreck
the clouds

Firmament

As far as the
eye can reach

The masts
bob

Ticking
against
firmament

Figure-head
speaking

Till the water
falls silent

Horizon

The horizon
lifted
upward

The mirror
of the sea
covered

The wreckage
jammed

Stubbornly time
drives on

Cloth

Should you
put out the image
line by line

It shrinks

The ebb dilutes
the image
to distance

The moon stretches
the cloth
to thirst

The fish ticks
against
the back

Transparent

With blotting-paper
you stick down
the horizon

To lose time
or the light's
shame

That quiet
transparency

Sealed
in white

Fisherman

Wires
stretched under water
Network
without meshes

No fish balances
on the nylon

The surface
divides the catch
No fisherman
who embraces the plankton

The haul
is the price
for the waiting

Pan
waits
behind the horizon

Windjammer

Moved by wind, always
the groaning wind
that begged
to be launched

Trees
bent in depth
alive
with seaweed and plankton

The belly full of stories:

*Up to the land
of the buffalo
we sailed!*

The sails
were the ship's
heart

The flapping
thoughts
of the nation

Shamelessly
stretched
on time

As far as
the eye could reach

And wind bowed
in lonely monologue

The painter visits the beach

These are the movements:
  walk(ing)
      sit(ting)
           look(ing)

A beachwalker, a stiltwalker
flies for the tide

Carefully the eyes muster
sometimes he raises his head

Speaks to the skylines
a far side within reach

His tongue hesitates
where the blue ends

Lisbon

Sometimes at night I dream of Lisbon
Slack diary elapsing in sun

Crumbling in outdoor cafés, white that
Discolours fast, the steps now taken

The mouth sealed, the parchment uvula
A rippling, the disguising that you are.

In vain the ship hauls up the bluntness inside
Saudade dissolves in affectionate tide

But the morning will not steer time
Comfort you think, but it doesn't

Still inhaling sleep, with the first sun
Sometimes at night I dream of Lisbon.

Bahia Blanca (Argentina)

Your dancing to keep up the thirst
The waving hair and scent that vaporises
A horizon there for the taking
A hut toppling over in the head

With bated breath I repeat the names
Of harbours as if I'm praying
Looking over your shoulder I see
The orchestra playing, your eyes:
My father dances a tango.

It was in an outdoor café in Bahia
– you don't dance the tango in Austria –
They turned you to wax: sun, bandoneon
Disappeared now and faded the caption

The hard times in your hand, the glass
You raised, your eyes that saw the powder
Breaking, cigarette smoke and lipstick
The voile of remembrance shaking the music:
My father dances a tango.

Asparagus, Asparagus
Felled by lust

Remember: the civilized patter, the steaming
Platters, the fat cigars, a crown apiece. The land
Of time, ready to oust the orange turnip.

Nothing: than the soft, the white, the taste
Of silver, holy wine. And the days grew longer.
The dancing voice of grass and wind

Interspersed the courses, called couples to the floor
Tangos and rumbas. Asparagus: discoloured joy
For the little boy hiding under auntie's ample dress.

These frigid fingers of darkloving death
Furtively bedded in blankness of sand
And shade, yet all too eager to touch and move.

Earthdrawn water in the hand
Of life, life arising, life aspiring
Without sound, from the void of underground

Queen of darkness, see your treasures
Torn. Felled by lust, rise up among the mist
Of morn: and face your sentence.

The land of dawn is in the earth
Turning the rich black clod. Lips are moistened
Always moist of mouth. Digging

For the hardened roots – defenceless –
She folds her hands in humble unison
Stoops demurely, moves her lips

To prayer, to desire. Lily warmth,
Exceeding tender flesh and celebration
Tears straight up the lower ground.

What makes it so translucent, so palatable
The tale of the golden ham –
Its delicate yellow crust.

The long table, the food, the evening. Candles
And the fondling breeze. The talk, delicate words
And the smile of wine. Nothing, only this

At the verge of time, on the grounds of life
Asparagus, asparagus, body and soul
Purging, dissolving. The smell of night forever.

No fast and loose in this: bleached
And bleached, whitest of white.
Signed and delivered, but melting.

Shy and dry: him liketh not the purple-headed
Hand-picked jewels of Lisbon, so defenceless,
The tough and tasteless joys of Long Island.

But yes, the juicy young buds from Peru,
Their heated shiver, caressing the inner skin,
The inner whisper swelling like a tropical totem pole.

After the days of pricks and parties
Autumn sheds its hues to the accompaniment
Of freesias, sad, discoloured, dying.

The season leaves her chilled: with ham
She wraps her shivering limbs: a whore,
She casts tough morsels to the tasteless.

Seamy stews of long gone journeys
Come sulking from the freezer.
Fallen she lies, irrevocably sad and broken.

Early Harbour

The groping hand that reaches out
And looks for warmth and youth
The landscape of good will
Limping and grimacing behind
The brass band: liberation

Dancing with ladies who left stains
Who kept sticking to mirrors
Like awkward butterflies
Fluttered with wings on their backs
Stitched down the uvula with their tongue
You hovered in a heaven of stiff tulle

Your teeth gnawed at your lipstick
Which later melted like a host on your tongue
During these scraping parties
The light flaked under the lamps
Sweat trickled down between her breasts
Making your hand slip along her chest.

Prayer for silent islands

He records a seeking, groping
Air, a litmus of his temper

He makes up light of permanence
Above the washed around land

A sea speech, though not compliant
In the self-contained water

He hears a voice changing
Its shingle or shell rests

Sometimes lapsing into dull sing-alongs
He sees the burdened water

The foam at the edge
'A yonder coast in winter storm'

And a weight of shadows full of stains.

Paricutin

The view slowly discolouring
In the morning haze round Paricutin

Her eyes black as lava, her bare
Feet dark, slow to come outside.

Her eyes dark as lava, against the
Desiccated wood, boarding up the soul.

Fir trees house dead branches of former
Headgear. Above the soaring, ever-

Plummeting eagle. A puzzled look prolongs
The silence of her appearance. A shadow

On the pumice path. I take a breath.
Cold air controls her disappearance.

The coastline shifts in mournful Stabat Mater.
You swallow mile on mile and fold

Your hands. Your croaking voice prays
To the God of Wings to remember

One feather burn and I'll return, to the place
At the foot of the volcano.

I want to stand looking out on the distance,
Wrest your hand from the shadow of night

Or horsehair bed. Soft as clay I wish to
Rest against your side and wait for the dawn

Remembering old lowlands, where the wind
Drives the ship onwards to these shores.

Terra Salsa

Lo there appeared a water
That wept joyfully in
All corners of the head
Nailed to the sand

And he saw the foam-headed
Sea hit the beach wildly,
Continually scouring
With bated breath

He surveyed the immense
Horizon, unending
Distance of the future

He slid into the breakers and
Bit the foam, tasted
The salty sweetness: as if he
Had not existed before, did

Not wish to be thereafter
Floating in Zeeland water
He entered his own dreams

Coasts of longing and sweltering
Dunes, throughout the night:
Island was what he wanted to be

Forever the step on the top
Of the dune, getting drunk
On water and air

Forever the fear of
Water and air, horizon
Making eyes smart, so tight.

Ripple

He grabs his old hands. A ripple towards death. Never
Again will he be big again. Never again will she be
Waiting round the corner. All words get lost. Everything
Had, has gone where? Now turn the prow for good and humour
The gondolier. Drink the wines, gulp down the yeasting
Beers. Soothe the hunger in the stomach. For redly on the
Quays lie the tough hooks of death.

Because everything

He stands in a distant country and pulls the flaking blue
Lime off the wall. Fresco of poverty, gesture of lacking
Power barrenly simulated. Civilization, you think, this
Mask of death eaten away by wind. This game without hope,
Before they break into hymns. Her clammy hand digs itself
Into his body. Because everything perishes. Desert wind,
This dog hour deadens.

*

Because everything perishes he deceives the night with
Unfinished Dreams. The yawning gods drink down their
Goblets. Idle speeches get hushed in the gnawing sunlight
And his shadow is smothered in sand. He breaks his self-
Image. A cactus hoists The backward look. Sailing in
Death-paper he catches his last breath and drinks until
His reaching lips touch on the worm.

*

Because everything perishes, only the precious remains in
Letters with barely legible handwriting. He beats fibers
Into paper in the hut of the old shaman blowing smoke
Over the past. He points to a distance of salt, no
Gesture or cool mouth. Barking shimmers in the air
When hunched the fire god doesn't fail to approach.

Blue agave

Stumbling over pigs. The ankles wrenching in the black
Dust, he neared the village, where fires still smouldered
And would not die out that night. Women vanished into
Their shadow horses whinnied. Gloomily the men gave way.
Only you knew who I was, when I came. Wordlessly you
Filled glass after glass. You sang for me until I fell
Asleep and dreamt of you, stumbling.

Farewell

Morning with translucent glaze, still blue with dew and
Head gasping for breath. Within a stone's throw from
The bow: You were still on my mind. So fondly scent
Keeps hovering in the head. So tenderly the gestures of
The farewell, the caresses preceding it. When wind skimmed
The board, the waves broke forward and the sight narrowed.

Sitting at the table

Sitting at the table, you
Eat, drink and sing a song

Death's cockscomb seems
Far, but ashes blow

Yesterday turns into today
Brief morning fades away.

*

Sitting at the table, you
Eat, raise your glass and drink

Wave smoke aside, light
a cigarette, match –

Sticks rattle, hairs
Fall into your soup. False

Nuts crack in their shells
Voices count slow strokes.

*

The years do not change
Bellies are filled, emptied

The carpet of guilt is swept
Your regrets cleansed, when

Door slam: the night
Is so oppressively low

No song here from your dear one.

In memoriam Lei Molin

Frail as a horizon in winter
With neither sea nor air, no voice left over

Lighter than a gull's feather, so sober
Whatever was blowing was less than wind

The light deprived of every colour
In cadence, forgotten water struck holes

Music faded at lingering tide. Seaman
Without ship, without bridge? Did you look back?

South Wall

In the middle of South Wall
Between rows of eternal limes
– Where did one see or find
  decay? –
The boy has returned

Playing with autumn leaves
Snow stuck to the shoes
Blossoms on his head
He walks kneedeep through
Meadow grass, sharp as nails

The arrows, the bow drawn back
The boy searches through the days
Stumbles when hail strikes
In his teeth, seawind blowing
Breaks the surface of the water

In his blue valise the boy hoards
Memories of roads and scapulars
Early neon bends the glass of the
Dream, he touches sinful saliva in
Leafy evenings. All lies waiting

On South Wall: the sea, the journeys
The mouldy odour of the night
The reversibility of the word
The mirage of death
And always a late hymn in the ear

Lips plump with kisses and memory of skin
Slumber, as yet unattached to language
Slowly touch the inner wall. Thus he
Imagines *her*, frenzied, impetuous, again and again
While gunsmoke drifts away

Father fills the glasses, the mother knits
In sadness. The boy bends the branches
Of heaven. And briefly he is back
Vanishes into himself and grows dim
In a future which passed long ago.

Brewhouse Farm

We never went to Uncle
Or Aunt, but to Brewhouse
Farm. A distant journey. Always
By bike, sitting behind my dad.

Hidden among trained limes and
Milk buses, in an outcorner
Of the Peel, we shouted hallo.
Thereupon they emerged into the yard.

A landscape of barren sand,
Scored by the centuries, not a word
In excess. A handshake, hot milk
Fresh from the cow, thereafter silence.

The town out of sight, a hand reaching
For the cockerel, the sharp bill hacking
At the child's shoe. Chickens clucking.
Water from pump and well. As if

Nothing would change. As if neither
Autumn nor winter would come,
The back of the horse hid
Nothing more than this quiet life.

Especially the mysterious smells
Of the farm, the pigs and the cows
That he tried to remember
At night, at home in bed.

Soft music sounded through the
Open bedroom window. Hilversum
Radio was a sea full of strange waves,
Rustling like wind in the limes. Smell

Got mixed up with sound, blending to
A solid memory of Brewhouse
Farm. Now gone, but sometimes still
With me, with no idea of time.

Divine spud

Was it on the IJzer or the Scheldt?
He must have walked there mouthing Flemish
A background of French, a thief up to his armpits.

He peacefully licked his wife out of sand
Drank away drought and carefully
Had his clods handled, past another war.

Thus decades later the miracle happened
Grandfather peeling and cutting the potato
Into slices and splitting them into strange stalks

Which he dried and sprinkled with salt in a
Place far from 's Gravenstenen. The brown pan
Waiting on the wood-fired stove.

Ox-fat heated to temperatures
That made him sweat right into his beer glass.
Angelus, the potato chips burbled in the

Razor of time, while the boy
Cycled each Friday till his lungs would burst
From his skinny body to avoid the nausea

Weekly caused by Catholic fish.
Gruesome God, how small his legs were
And how big the hunger on days when the plates

Steamed a golden yellow, salt was added
Like an elixir and the divine spud crisply
Touched his milk teeth: teeth chewing peacefully

In a sea of salutary saliva, the tame pigeon
Watching on his shoulder, and he shifting
The cap on his bald head saw that it was good.

Divine spud II

They ate you since
There was nothing –
Huge was the iron cauldron
Sparse the green-grey light

Of the oil-lamps, you lived
Blotchy in your skin –
Thus they devoured you.

You cut off an ear or stuck
A knife in the pig. You lay
In blood and dank autumn

Lament of edibility in
A gobful, saliva of
Hunger and every death, they ate you –

You were a prole between
Zeeland Clay and Beste Borgers
A changeling in sandy soil

You found a home in sand
Looking breathlessly for water
To feed yourself

Shunning the sun
Clad in shabby leaves
Forever awaiting rain

You grew in armpits of clay
Wordless to the no-light
Of stomachs. Rough to the touch

Of the reapers. Next you steamed
In plain pans and you disappeared
In coarse bellies round the moor

Sometimes you appeased the ravenous
Sorrow of shy lovers
And kissed shameless tongues.

Well, sand groveller, I always
Took you carefully from the
Potato bin and cherished your purple

Skin. Far into spring you
Remained the saviour of
An unheard child.

In your velvety crumbs
You rose from your death in
A mouth that champed, crunched

Like a tango record from the dark
Days of the Colorado beetle
Oh, lost future of the past.

I meet you everywhere in a plurality
Of innocence. Unwashed you lie
Shamelessly for sale on damask

Tablecloths. A pustular landscape
Of starch curves under the hands
Of the jetset in Le Madri, N.Y.

They feel you. They snigger and
Wipe their hands. They sit down
And empty plates and all there is.

No, this was not the glorious
Return of a displaced person, but
A violation of bitter longing.

Nehalennia

The rushing of waves in the night
The windless expanse at low tide and
The soft snapping of foam, thus

Tasted the caviar of her mouth,
Thus she rose from the dark deep
Where she lay hidden on her

Altar, among waving weeds and
Mussels, hardening on her stone
To a pustular oblivion.

She waded in luminous foam
And dried herself on marram
Her feet were resting on the

Bitter moss of the dunes and we
Sang songs from those days,
Hips shook in the night.

She looked and motioned me away –
Not minding burnet-rose and sand-white
Lunar image, when she disappeared into the sea.

In December, when time stands still,
Memories pull like dogs at
Their chains, grains of salt

May powder your hair. The altar
Of your thighs has been silent for ages
And is scoured by the tide.

We no longer sing those songs
Of yore. The sea is cold,
A fixed object for icy wind.

Only at spring tide you still
Show your light, a courtesan
Mounting the beach during

A winter storm. The days, the
Dog days, have passed you
By. All fruits are petrified –

And yet, setting my course, I
Reach for your cold hand and taste
The brine of years.

Trees

Always the trees there
They harbour in heads
Their crowns in the wind
They wave in nests

The grain of memory
Their breathless story
In peat, in carbon
Black trees, petrified

Bark conceals time
Skin is a silence
A tear in the water
Of the rain, oh

*

The trees, they slumber
In the night, pulling
At dreams, withdrawing their
Roots from our existence

Topple their headgear
Concealing decay
The trees, the trees
So close in the night

Sing of their leaf-sea
Embark you on a stream
Of wind, and read me:
How I have loved you.

Since all must pass

I shall lift the tears from your eyes
Kiss the salt from your cheek
Be silent about the death of day
And dusk against your skin

Since all must pass

I shall allow the wood and the fires
Steal a feather from your head-dress
Reach for the beaker and leave the smoke
Till water burns and wait.

Adíos pampa mío

In daytime the head is nestled
In wind it meekly mourns
Sun is a bilious headache
Thirst a scanty trust

Waiting for the dance, the sun-hat
Leans back against the palm
Drought tasting of mescal
Her shoulders compelling eyes

His boot hesitantly touching
Wood, her tongue licking
The level of smell, he reads the sand
Around her feet, offering her his verse.

Milonga

This is a toe or heel dance
A slalom in movement which
Stirs, spoons up and congeals
On the tip of a toe, a foot
Sweating in a shoe

Fastening itself on the floor
And falling in love languidly
Kissing breasts, licking sweat
Falling back into wise nagging
In order to stir, to spoon up

With toe and heel between thigh
Legs which lifted up from the
Floor, are floating, coming down
And stand candle-like on stiletto-heels
In barren violating pampas.

Walker

While he walks,
Making that
Movement, kissing the skin of a larch,
With faded tangos in his voice,
The lake yawns and belches.

A mandolin strums out a part song
Of foot and distance, while he
Walks his track is no doubt
Fußgeist, an insole in the shoe.

While he walks, writing is
An empty gesture in space
A smirk in open air
A flight away from walking –

While he walks – He walks –

A sin in a far region, stilling
Distance step by step. The grit
Scuffs and shakes the bit. Acidity slows
The muscles. Heavy legs, heavy legs

Sings the chorus of the arrogant. He
Walks, without time or hour to the
Finish. His silence is dumb at the
Line, that finish well-remembered.

Get lost, curses footwear, scumbag –

While he walks.

Mondrian in Domburg

On the beach, legs crossed,
Arms bent, he sits without moving
And catches wind for his trees.

Leaf-fall sinks below the horizon,
Ship's sail confuses him just
—This is a later life —

High tide encircles in broad ovals,
Rains screens an early summer,
Old views shrink and are lost.

★

Singing the salty psalms
Under church stones polished red:
You dismantle their song. Benches

Crossed your path. You disbanded
The crossbeams, till bright light
Fell on the canvas and pure

Music rushed through your ears. In
The Spa Pavilion that night you
Danced new patterns on the floor.

Sierra Bermeja

You want that red that blasts from the soil
Sweltering with death and stripes from
Castigating the days. Orange yellow
That stains and lightens the canvas skies

You cut through the edge of the rocks. Pure
And simple the evening comes, even there.
In the Sierra blue thunders, barking
And howling so closely to the dog hour.

The sweaty sheet lies chalk white and
Crumpled on the floor. You pull
The grass from your forehead. Once more you blast
Speech in all colours from the soil.

Misanthrope

In the lost huts of memory
Which once were the future, he hides
Under his broad-brimmed hat
Of distrust, the recluse.

His ink stains
The Poor paper which curls at
The Edges and cockles in places when
Touched tenderly, carefully

He doubts in his skin of paint;
For once put down in that place
Time will smoulder in dead leaves
And ceaseless scoffing will not do.

Don Quixote in landscape

Always the edge is too low, too wide
But by no means high enough. Lonesome
Knight with pointed lance, the distance
Is a lonely search, an assault

On thirst, a deadening of
Speech and the sand which everywhere
Like news that scratches slows down time,
Haunts imagination in a mime.

In the shimmering plain the mill lies.
Half-lit canvas hides the view.
He comes ever closer. Never yet has
She got lost in him.

Itamaracá, *the song of Fort Orange*

Perhaps an orange glow, in a sun emptied of light.
Tired water that scours stone. Low tide laps
The coir of coconuts. And there's far-off
Itamaracá, the old sails, the battlements,

Guns silenced in sand. The balls and the
Bones. Fort Orange cherishes sand over
Servile past. Barely touched when
Evening falls, and the sea tells

Her old story. Bare feet on the
Beach. Dancing in foam that splashes
Cheerfully up to the moon, while she kisses
The eyes closed, reproachfully licks the lashes.

Cape Death

Cabo da Morte / Galicia

The mimosa yellow scent of January
You are camellia tar with me
The day gnaws under the armpits
Eucalyptus wood steams
In the long, long evening

This is no farewell note
Haughtily placed in a bottle
Surrendered to the evening air –
Perishing knows no time –
But now that the ship lingers

Current brushes the anchor in vain
Farewell lies on the lips –
I see that boat, that ship –
Filmy words rustle, tide strikes
The already wet sand, stabs

The barb into the lip of this
Cold master, breakers mirror
Your hand. I cradle this journey's head
In dead sails, surrender it
To the evening air.

Descriptions of the lake

Describing the lake
You forget the mountains, the trees
And the water. Boats lie
Tilted above the floodline. The
Island is a mirage.

Describing the lake
Fish laugh dry tears,
Rock crumbles like dry rye bread
In the birds' nests of yesteryear.

Describing the lake
The colours fade from a postcard
To be diluted into sad cups.
Describing the lake
        It snows for days on end.

Describing the lake
The water wells over the edge and
Puts out the fire under the iron
Pots. The sand is blackened,
Honey seeps from the evil eye.

Describing the lake
You hear tin-kettle music and
Open a packet of lard. Lightning
Splits trees and stone.

Describing the lake
Ships sail through the evening
And beer turns flat in the barrel.
Describing the lake
      Soot falls from the skies.

Describing the lake
You hear thin tango music and
Draw more closely to the light. The day
Refuses to turn to night. Sleep
Is a shameless disgrace, for

Describing the lake
You cut fields of cloud from blue
Napkins and bodies are steaming pink
Until they congeal under a marigold leaf

Describing the lake
The ice fields await and the
Consul dies in a tub full of mescal.
Describing the lake
        A soft chord sounds from the tarropatch.

Describing the lake
A waterfall descends in foam
And he considers the latest lines in
His face. The dry grimace
Of a pig's bladder. Rumble-pot.

Describing the lake
Chaff turns into grain and bull-rushes
To old gin, undrinkable. You were always
An old fool. Rattletrap.

Describing the lake
You smell oilskins, plastic and
Blue and acts of contrition.
Describing the lake
      He rises and walks again.

Describing the lake
The palm rests on the water, and
Carp and bream suck soft as silk.
Voluptuous lips, the tender
Innocence of a hand. Uncalloused.

Describing the lake
You died every day over your
Glass of sputum. Bye bye Clareyn.
For a moment you surface again.

Describing the lake
I still see your careful shuffle,
Counting each step with your eyes.
Describing the lake
      I stir ashes into your gin glass.

Describing the lake
Old and dead friends dance
A kolo. A ribbon of glass and eye
Sparkling, the future so
Far off and time to spare.

Describing the lake
Delusions turn to morning haze and
Thinly vanish. Donkey on
The hill, a vessel full of treacle.

Describing the lake
The potholes of Sveti Naum claim
The poets and all their verse.
Describing the lake
        Mouths sift the sand.

Describing the lake
Fits a grimace, a letter to the
Editor by Elb cussedly rowing with
Impatient oars. Dusk of the gods
'Seething like suds' 'Ping ping'.

Describing the lake
I carefully avoid the salt water,
Only kiss the sweet, the bowl of
The tramp, the lead of the bullet.

Describing the lake
The shot is still the heart of the
Poem, dead-accurate desire.
Describing the lake
        The decoy duck honks.

Describing the lake
Fingers turn cold as ice
And murder and death rest close
To the heart's wall. Each night
Is brutally beheaded there.

Describing the lake
White wind sweeps across the fields
And hands you water, till your throat
Downs it and sinks deeply into isolation.

Describing the lake
Blood is wiped out, wounds are
Healed and fringes repaired.
Describing the lake
      Equals a scraggy carcass.

Islands

Meandering in a landscape
Of rapeseed and gloomy
Woods. Death. And rushing cloud-
Depressions across the rocks.
Darkness of the past and the
Island which he
Clung to, like one drowning
To the side of a ship.
And lightning above.

Always that person, his shadow
Wherever you go, pass by.
Silent stranger. Seeing
Stagnation in the water,
A reflection. Doppel-
Gänger laying his hand
On the evening and next on the
Sinking ship, lost
Eye of the night.

As the island floats so the fish
Swims. Wind fails and the
Canvas dreams itself into
The next century. Your
Print in the white sand,
Without footstep no departure.
Birds on air and all around is sound
From ear to ear. As the fish swims
So the island floats.

Evening light *(Maastricht)*

With the child he watches
The water and the arches of the bridge.
Before him just the streets of
The town, worn reflection in the
Stream, dream that lapsed.
Walking across the squares, through
The seasons. Autumn drenched in rain
And the sad eyes of churches. The old
Stones give comfort in this the last
Of months, when the water whirls
Wildly and the wind drives.

Down wintry steps you descend
To the river, the child lost
Behind words. Hidden in
'Sea Memory', your face and
Dusk on the embankment. My hand
Writes on the water: departure is
Waiting for a return, always it is
Getting later. A final look, the town
Shines in the rain. I embark in
The evening light. Vanish on the
Stream, repeating the question
When will I meet you again?

Maas / Meuse

Sweet water, then salt
And back again, that is what
The Maas wants, flowing

Through the rolling landscape.
Lovely like a silvery eel,
Chaste like Stella Maris.

Mother of the salt
And the sweet, blessed be
The ships full of wine and

English fun.
Blessed Maastricht,
Rimbaud's ghost,

The wet backs of the
Stations of the Cross and
Veldeke's stone statue.

But equally the Maas
Wants bridges, spectacular
Bridges under which

Her wintry aspect
Whirls. And suicides
Throw themselves

Into shining picture
Postcards of self-deception
And flowing water. Even the

Dry white wine of Slavante
Is what the river wants to
Become breath of the sea,

A ghost of itself. Always
Paddling cheekily in an
Ever-changing counter-stream.

Leaf, leaves

I recognised the man who kissed
The lips of death, wiped
A love from his brow.

I saw him balance on the
Ice floes of angular
Splinters and heavenly snow.

Soaked in nocturnal sweat, the
Scratching of pencils, of
Begging and swearing on paper.

Until the cloth fell, the curtain
Was torn and the light shone
White and pale under the skin.

Down to the bone. Agony
Shining through, which wrapped
Itself up and vanished.

The man who faced the Styx, and
Next the hay, the wool, the feathers and
Her whom he called *Ginkgo Biloba*.

Across the fields

Across the fields, well past the midst
Of life, the shadows of the paths.
The changing of the harsh afternoon light.
A feather in his throat and watching

Things tumbling slowly. Across the fields
The word strides, so slowly that sound
Loses itself, dissolves in the mist over
The stubble fields. And the walker? He

Peers across the fields at the fading
Horizon. Tries to step out of his
Shadow, while dusk falls around
His head. The dead rustle among

The autumn leaves or rest on the branches
Of the past. If there should be a farewell,
Let it wait and bring a little 'wood
To the forest and peat to the moors'.

Galway

We smelled the smoke in the pubs, gazed
At the peat fires, as if everything would
Last and nothing had changed. Words
Unspoken, suppressed, left in the dunes,

On beaches. Perhaps, you said,
There are journeys one takes alone, if we
Lived without time or need. But wherever
The roads went, ships arrived and I

Looked for your face in every port.
Horizons are but a perspective, ever in
A different light. You voice is parched, you said.
Come here and put your lips to glass or verse.

Aran Islands

The ferry to the islands cleft the waves.
The holy water swept in from the Atlantic
Across the edges of the bay. A gale
Intertwined our hair and grains of salt

Filled the lines of years. A hand
Covered a hand. Stacks of peat rose
In our heads. Like a pig being
Stuck or crumbling black pudding on

Our plates, steaming amidst apples and
Autumn. But isn't it spring, you said and
Hummed an old tune in my ear. We stared
At the proud waters of the luminescent sea.

Sailor's legs felt for the quay. A
Lame duck waddled from the ship. A near-
Dead man was lying on the quay. Drunk, dropped
Out of his frame, tongue still grey with whiskey,

Erosion of Jameson on the lips. Today this is
Our island, you said and pulled me away from
Him. Salt rain corroded the houses. There
Were no trees to carve one's name in.

Grey the skies, grey the water. No hangover
Lurking here. We gazed across the forgotten
Islands, where stone rules over the dead
Unintelligibly, and the day contracted.

Shivering we covered ourselves in blankets.
The horse's hoofs clacked steadily,
As if the roads were soft paths, every
Step reversible. Seals were swimming

Towards the horizon. Potatoes lay like
Eggs in the scanty peat. On your lips
I tasted the salt that encrusts stone,
And then you looked at me, looked back

Through my eyes. This is the end of a world,
You said, where old can never age. Where
Time is silence in an urn filled with ashes. Aran,
Dream with the smell of horse blankets.

On the death of a Colorado · 580 kg

The playing field seemed open. Someone
Stuck a rosette into your side,
Like being decorated
By the land of grass, and its endless

Grazing and sun in which you
Ruminated so contentedly, and breathed,
That put you to rest, your tail swishing
On green pompadour. The sliding

On your entry from the vaults of the
Arena. Your eyes blinking and squinting.
Chasing the agitators back behind the
Red wooden screens. The sandy plain

Yours for just a while.
Sand grates between your hooves.
Then iron spear stabs, splinters
Spine, nerves and tendons.

Stubborn anger weeps deep inside.
Blood seeps, streams down
The sides. Drips, drips
The red that reddens voluptuous

Lips. The hairy tongue bulges,
Promiscuous covenant. While
Banderillas are caught in
Pairs in the skin. But you

Breathe young grass, playmate,
Ogle the dance master who
Calls you and you nod and look
And you advance a step or

Retreat, blood dripping, foam
At the mouth. Your tail stuck
Up and wagging. This rugged
Body must be filled with sadness,

Nostalgia for those green days,
The caresses, in the eager
Light. You watch, panting, your head
Registers disbelief. But the

Ballet dancer focuses on your back,
Finds the spot, judges the distance
On the tips of his toes. And you,
Colorado, bend your head, scrape

A hoof as if undecided. Good
Fortune is unerring. Up to the hilt.
Blood cough, death rattle. Down.
A dream of endless grass and grazing.

THE ROCK 'N' ROLL POEMS

The Days before Rock 'n' Roll

Just you try, wearing odd-coloured socks,
Dancing promiscuously before the
Gates of Hell and the Waste Land, drinking or
With beer streaming down between the legs

Of The Killer. On the Road and ever-
Changing music. Life was so simple and
Work must be done. Words kept spinning
In your head and radio stations whirled

In your ear like pollen. The world glowed like
A green cat's eye in the living room. When I
Turned the tuning knob I listened to forbidden,
Repeatedly forbidden music, and there was no

Sorrow, there was no death. And photographs had
Scalloped edges and showed cheerful seaside scenes.
Him in dark sunglasses. Him showing off in
Swimming trunks and both feet stuck in quicksand:

***

Johnny Weissmuller in cheap cotton swimwear.
Roy Orbison plunging into the waters of Zeeland.
Hello Dad, you old fogey, are you still
There? Come on, hard worker, sly tippler,

God's Witness of the eternal gin! On rare
Occasions we raise our glasses and something
Gleams in the shadow of a spotless white shirt,
A gold cufflink, in which you are lost.

Bill Haley in Maastricht

What had not assailed the ears!
The dulcet tones of Mantovani, Helmut Zacharias.
Sugary syrup of the lowest seaside sort. Incestuous
Family gathering. Hurrah for raised skirts.

The grasping, groping hands. The uncles
Heated, randy with lager and provocative drops
Of gin. Catholic orgy, suddenly smothered
By Bill Haley and his whirling cornets.

Their sound burst into the room like
Exploding shells. As if the devil himself had
Appeared. As if the end of time had come
And the curtains were torn to shreds.

Never were heads shaken so firmly and was
Spittle blown to all points of the compass.
One of those days, filled with dire curses,
Sleepless nights and snoring daydreams.

★★★

Time languishes in vinyl, like sad banknotes.
Yes, the spit curl stuck to his forehead. Yes,
Blue jeans blew their top. Fat-bellied
Rock 'n' Roll, with Moluccans swinging and

The bass player bestriding his instrument.
Pints were downed, disappearing in the
Hollows of everyone's past. Bill Haley
In Maastricht. Late Sunday service, Brylcreem

On old heads. Their fathers, already dead,
Had to be reburied. Steam rising
Once again. I turned my back on those fragile
Days: SHAKE RATTLE 'N' ROLL.

The last waltz

Had I forgotten you in stereo sound?
Dolby, Dolby, in that square in Amsterdam?
The Schiller Hotel, floating on the past
Like a cabin cruiser. I was asked to show

My singing diploma, paint my
Masterpiece – you would not take less,
Madame, and touch down in Brussels.
As if streets were flown in from Rome

With me painting clowns' faces on
Non-existent covers. For a moment I
Was in Venice with you, sailing in 'a dirty
Gondola' to the dead of yesteryear.

***

When Time proved an impertinence. We
Drank prosecco to this tender reunion and
Later dreamt of frayed ends hanging like
Wisps of hair over the celluloid.

Sound full of noise and scratches. But whenever
Your tongue waltzes in my ear and the first bars
Sound once again, the old dance resumes,
Madame, and everything spins as of old.

Yonder, to Ghent

The old man from a past that will always
Remain past. In long grey streaks, the
Shifting colours of memory.

There was nothing yet, just a vague
Hint of excitement,
A restless longing for the trip,
The distance that would be achieved.

The land of my grandfather in
A majestic distance, stories
Meandering through the boy's
Head, restless, in a rolling surf

Of prayers. Sinful language deep
In the ear and the girls over there.
Excited by conjectures.
There was nothing yet, avoiding

A paving stone, playing hopscotch.
Burgeoning fair, peeping timidly,
In a church full of pain, organ, absence.
There was nothing yet, just the dream.

But Ghent was his life, so Grandad said.
Sweat pouring from under his cap, slurping
His brandy and eating cow udder. Migrant
Avant la lettre, world pigeon fancier.

Pint on the table, dancing on hands
And feet and the prevailing mores bald
Like his head. Brown nicotine on his
Tongue. Underneath a layer of empty

Bottles of pain. But breezy and irascible.
Blowing like an old satyr, longing
For the past, a return, and never no more.
His grandson in his town? He prayed

A rosary of glasses, or talked
Of his bayonet, the attack. A
Death, as ever, in the offing. But
I wanted to go yonder, to Ghent.

The boy standing there, with the biggest
Eyes in the world, his dry mouth full
Of wonder. May God have a photo of this
Simpleton, this waking Lamb of God.

Nourishing himself at the breasts of the
Naked Eve. Drank Piedbœuf, smoked
Lucky Strike and Chesterfield from
The harbour where Uncle Jeff,

Loving uncle, gauged ships. In
Town pointed out those lovely
Ghent girls and said that I should not just
Feast my eyes in St Bavo's.

And think, 'Ans, think and reflect
Again. Life is too short to let it
Pass. Uncle Jeff's first tears.
I watched him with the largest eyes

In the world. Think, he said again.
By thinking I have thought myself dead and
Woke up naked under a pile of bodies.
By thinking I have thought myself to life again.

Closing his blue eyes for a bit he stroked
My head. Each to his own war, he said
Softly. Your grandad had his war,
The great war. He also survived this one.

At his local pub he cracked jokes,
Drank English ale as if nothing had
Happened. Nothing would ever happen again.
Life had been lived. He would light

Another St Michel. Inhaled
Deeply and blew out the smoke of the
Green dragon through nose and mouth.
'Next stop Big Bertha.'

In wakeful sleep, topography that
Slowly unfolded. Grandad in buses
And trains. Yonder, to Ghent. To
Bury his father. But every time

Got lost at stations. I met him again in
Smoke-stained bars: corpse among corpses,
Boozer among boozers, dreamer
Among dreamers. A week after the funeral

He was staggering across Cornmarket.
'Oh for those days' I wrote later. The
Smooth shit holes of Ghent Castle,
The bashful skeletons of girls with velvety

Brown hair attached to bone. Black iron
Of the torture chamber. Passing Breendonk
'You see, my boy,' he cried. 'Life is
A ship listing unexpectedly.'

'My knowledge is supported by death.
Smell the old wood and know that
Your future once began with my father.'
The old man from a past that will always

Remain past. In long grey streaks, the
Shifting colours of memory and
Questions that remain questions. Hearing
Pigeons coo I think of Ghent, of them.

Uncle Jeff struck down by the green
Dragon and Grandad finally dropping.
From toilet bowl onto the floor.
My God, how dead he must have

Been, lying there on the floor,
Fingers bent, clotted blood
On his head and nobody there,
Nothing and cold, so bitterly cold.

MAASTRICHT PUB CRAWL

La Vierge

But we knew not that the Virgin was

Finite, would vanish. We tried every
Worn-out image: snow, sun, autumn,
Winter, summer. But the Virgin vanished
As if she had never been. Month after month

We searched for the countless glasses, countless
Beers, spicy sausages, the songs we didn't
Always appreciate, yet joined in quietly
When the heavy beers Westmalle or Duvel
Or Petermanneke made themselves felt.

No mourning cards were sent out. The hop
Round the entrance grew rank. Dust blew from
The letterbox, dust of uprooted customers and their
Lost stories. Reader, do not pass this place
Without remembering them in drunkenness.

Café 't Haantje

Shoes polished to a deep black shine,
Pomade like a wet helmet covering the scalp.
When she rose from her pub stool, caught
His arm, muttered a summons:

'C'mon lad.' And how she twisted, he smelled
Her intoxicating armpit. Kissed that
Dark-haired labyrinth and was lost
In a maze of steps. 'Accordéon!'

Among bar stools and tables, heaven
Gained, hell lost. Sweat, drops of
Needling salt. Her tongue in his ear.

People watching, talking, drinking
And smoking. World peace spread
Over the Market Place, unto far-away Liège.

Tribunal

How the revolutionary fire did burn and cause
An itch in those days and make the temperature
Rise. How the painter Harrie B.,
At the same time Chairman of
The Lowlands Weed Company,

Offered me, after Police Terrorisation &
Incarceration the first liberated glass of
Beer at the Tribunal Pub and asked: How
Is your work getting on? You see, you don't
Forget Harrie. He is the sand in the Sahara's

Memory. He is the accomplice of
The camels. Mirror of eternal sunshine and
Sad WhamBam. Harrie who, smoking calmly
Between camel's legs, invented the Gothic Age
While it rained desert sand and later on he

Found he was slowly drowning. In Casablanca
He suddenly appeared at my side, brushing the rim
Of my borsalino. We drank sweet tea.
Life had got lost. The future held
No prospect. We wiped the forbidden beer

From our lips. We stared through
The window-shutters, stretchers without canvas.
His window-shutters that looked out from
White light. Breathing against
Frozen glass, the frost flowers disappeared.

Walker

Where were you walker, on the day
You died? Crying with your head
Down on moss and regret like an island or
Were you out cold in a bar?

Were you hiding there snivelling? While
Tears of old times filled the glasses,
Full shot glasses touched your lips trembling
For sorrow is huge and will ever have more.

Where were you dodderer, on the day
Your wooden coffin was nailed down? Seven
Streets to the sea and always seven streets back.
There you lounged in other arms and danced

Six beats. You had six glasses of rum and moaned
Against the bar, while everyone was waiting for you
Sadly. But you, as always, did not give
A damn, you drunken sot, abandoned corpse.

'I lay down in the Citadel, dreamt of velvety
Virgins, but found none.'

Did you cut cherry wood, with a loose
Chisel and useless hinge? A passion for words
Spoilt the fun to the last degree.
Bye walker, mandarin of latter days.

Wine is a mocker

Mother of Comfort, bands undone
On the ground, shoes lost,
Shot satin shifted.

Her breasts exposed, even
Her bum. Lying on a wheelbarrow
For centuries. Her head, pink,

Full of surprise, sleeps the dream of
Drunks. Her stockings, red,
Blaze in ignorance of

Laughter and mockery. Whom
She kissed, which songs she
Sang and how many rummers of wine

She had? Perhaps she danced
On the table, before tumbling outside.
Mother of Consolation, resting

In drunkenness, stilled
In wine, your lips full of mercy
Mockery cannot touch you.

Studio

Brush lacking a hand. The roofs of the
Hills rest on the children. The car
Is a splash of paint gone by.

There is no waking now nor
Sleeping or slumbering at the piano.
The journeys smoulder in your ashes. Without

Home your paintings, desk, and all
That you were. What seemed so firm
Faded away. White canvas was left,

Snow in strict ranks against
The wall. Nothing, just your voice
There, on the answerphone.

A distant noise. Memory
Of a time when days did not
Count and your eyes would still

Sparkle like wine from Ronda,
Gran Reserva. The way you drank
Down life, to the lees.

Going down slow

And then there were those days, the colours
Still fixed in your head, and chests full of
Memories. There were those days at Helle,
The days filled with lasses and with books

And our three girlfriends, dancing
At the Prado. The sweet gelatine of their
Thighs. You counting the dimples with tapping
Draughtsman's fingers and your ever-caressing

Artist's eye. And there were those days
When asparagus was cut and
Grimly dispatched and washed down with
White wines, trucked in in small

Tankers from the Alsace. Thus we drank
Through the days in friendship, told
Our stories, read paintings, painted
Poems: panoramas without years.

Glass

It was glass, soft glass
That shone in your hands.

Glass shining dimly, glass
Waiting for the wines

Of summer. Everything blew
Glass, every second

Shone. When death
Touched shirt sleeve.
Summer fall. Winter vigil.
    Nightfall.

SALTY TEARS OF YOUTH

Dad,

Many years and some months have passed.
I am now that man you could
Have been, alive. The same paunch,
Curly waves on the barely balding head,
The constant silence, feet on the table
And always runny eyes. Your glass. Older.

Wherever we were there was a distance, a
Gruff doggedness. You kicked your eldest son
Wherever you could: ankles, calves, shins.
Usually under the table or in church.
Invisible torture until the soup spoke up.
The smooth slurping began.

Dad,

This is a night to remember
Things. Things I know about you,
The smallest things, now lost forever.
The smacks from an angry hand, the head
Spinning against walls and the everlasting
Scolding of the woman that fed your blows.

I became the silent one you had been and she
The widow for Ever & Aye. The vitriol
Of Trouble & Strife. There was no answer.
You hid yourself in your gold rings and gilded
My milk tooth, which later adorned your tie.

Dad,

I do not now remember your voice. Just
A vague dissatisfaction, mainly a low
Rumbling in mid-distance. But I recognise
You at parties singing along with your
Amsterdam hero, without a tie.
The raised shot glass in your hand,

Your face tilting and perspiring,
Singing lustily, your eyes shining.
The days knew no end. You inhaled
Life. Every Sunday God was close,
As in Old Mac (85 cents), Lexington,
And finally Caballero (packets of 25).

Dad,

We have never had a good cry together,
Folded each other in our arms,
Or touched each other's cheeks,

Unless it was the rasping kiss on
Your stubble cheek before
Going to bed – she insisted.

And all those years when you were
A paragon of propriety.
My God, Dad, did you never have

A day when you dreamt about
Those women under your hands?
About tender cheeks or soft breasts?

Dad,

You settled with her at the till with
Or without change. Numbered the days.
You stared through the walls as if you

Smelled death, your head was crumbled.
Your eyes pools of water, in which
The past oozed, leather strops

Thrashing your deathbed. I recall you
Once again: you were older
Than I was and younger than I am.

We might have lifted out hats to
Each other graciously, decayed
Gentlemen on a beach in Zeeland.

Mother

Etched on the membrane that endears
The tympanum to us, recording so
Accurately, clinging closely to memory –

Nostrils quivering and hands
Transmitting nocturnes wrapped in
Foliage – she was like granite.

A mother of scrap fights,
A mother like a bronze statue
That wanted to be loved, kissed;

That melted at the warming
Of a flat iron. In the fury
Of her world the ambulance

Turned out, sirens wailing,
To remove her in a straitjacket.
Let us pray, said the father, that she

May receive her just punishment
And only then realised that one of his sons,
He who was closest to the eldest,

Spat flames at him, before vomiting
Heavily and colourfully on her
Tablecloth embroidered with roses.

Slow approach

Bones buried that are no longer
Relevant. Her skin lost. Where are
The caresses, your mouth on my
Cheeks? Kiss me Mother, kiss me.

Every day your love chafes
Like a burn. Though time no longer
Matters. I concede, Mother, I give in,
I harden the cold image that will

Look back. I am down on a doorstep,
Crying. There is no home but our old one.
Dragged across by the ears. Don't

Kick up a fuss. Mother, my bed
Is no longer my old bed. Between your
Breasts I am always and ever yours.

Altar boy

Only I myself remember who you were,
Fair-haired boy, little altar boy
With your blue eyes, six years old.

Your hands folded and head
Bent. Kneeling in a black cassock
And a white surplice on the bottom

Altar step. Ringing the bell. Praising
In pure Latin the Mother of God.
Confessing guilt. Pronouncing Credo.

As if all was Soap-proof Sunlight
You retched while swallowing the
Blood-drenched corpus that

Had first stuck to your tongue like
A white rash. Each wafer was dying
In dreams of fire and pains of hell:

Fair-haired boy, little altar boy.
I now look back at you, with
Mature eyes, the hands not folded.

Eat the leavened bread, lick
The altar wine from your fingers and
Fear no more. Yet you are still so

Near that sometimes I taste the salt
Of your boy's tears. Recognise your
Look and memorise the years.

Dead poet

I carry a dead poet in my mind,
He no longer speaks my words, has
Got lost in language, his word is
Cold, vicious and knife-blue.

I carry a dead poet in my mind,
His mug is ashen grey, still full of
Late-night drunkenness, nightly
Remorse and deadly sorrow.

I carry a dead poet in my mind,
A body holed with letters. Teeth
Tired of biting, his hands so worn:
I carry a dead poet in my mind.

Azul

When we were part of that region –
The sea so close, with the sand, dry
And damp, smelling of sand – did
The child's head bend and lie down.

I was the early sleeper and my
Voice gargled in sea shells. I was
The prophet of the sea, with sand,
With spade and lugworm in my hand.

I was a childhood image, gnawing
The break of day, trouble-free beach.
When we were part of that region –
Tide rising, no escape –

Did the water reach my lips.
I had become the waves, the child
Of those days. The land with holes
In the clouds, fingers at the edge.

Budapest 1956

A word is a word and next the word curls
Like a vine leaf full of lice, forgotten scum.
Deadly fungus that spares house nor home.

Memory shouts in contradiction, but what is
Memory? A rag to polish antique brass?
Grandparents dead, while Pest raged.

The Danube full of blood. Budapest hanging
From lampposts. The Russians shooting.
Mindszenty in my dreams. Empty

Mumbling and always that cardinal's face
From the magazine. Inside my head
I couldn't but disown my hands.

Submissive heads. Not knowing
Differently. A choral song of forgiveness
And a double somersault for everything

That flowed down the river: blood sloshing
Against the banks like a Viennese waltz.
Why were those television screens so grey?

Il Castello di Duino

I was looking at myself in my eye,
Removing fine dust with cotton buds.
Entered by the main entrance to the castle.

I could hear Rilke sigh, limping across
Round stones, perhaps arm in arm
With the pretty farmer's wife providing

A hold on the vaulted 'Salone delle conchiglie'.
Here one could ponder on Fatherland,
Guitar and Sea and the Murmur of Waves,

Bitter, disturbing thoughts. A bedroom
That was not there while I was looking. Violins
That I saw but did not hear. Poems that

I found but could not read. Orphaned language.
As tears were dripping wet letters, which were
Unwept, there in the heart of Duino.

Polskie tango

The wooden extension of the village pub.
Inside the cast-iron stove, breathing
Fire, drying the washing, dreaming of stars.
There she's singing tangos. Her voice scratches

From the grey grooves of the record. What's
Bothering you, she asks and licks his earlobe.
He kisses her fingers and hugs her so
Tightly in a Polskie Tango that their bodies

Bond, she raises her leg and commits
Herself. Pepper vodka is ordered. Oh my
God, a tango is not a march to war.
This is stalking foot by foot, in intangible

Time. This is sweetly singing falsetto in dark
Glasses. This is stopping the years, because
The dead are still alive. Drinking a glass
In the village pub, listening to her,

Who kisses drunks, offers comfort, furtively
Brushes his fly buttons. Where tears become
Salt crystals. Hand touches bosom.
Black Madonna, may I have this dance?

For the love of women

There is the sea and you're back again,
As if time is an ivory boat, a
Silver cigarette case or tie-pin,
With the old bunkers still booming.

A Cold War despot threatens.
The barmy barrow boy peddling his
Wares in dancing polyps in the
Post-war years. Mother hoarding her

Quiet treasures, flour, the sunny sunlight
Soap. Preserves fruit. Churns milk. Skims
Off butter. A sudden fright at the black-edged
Envelope on the doormat. Unsolicited, unsent.

There is the sea and you're back again,
Slack water, troubled water, tasting oysters.
Remembered salt and cheap wine. You spit,
Gargling the years gone by on the shell path.

I may turn into brine, may turn into water.
Or into ashes in the sand-coloured deaths of
My friends. Mayonaise de la Flandre,
Prawn croquettes, and Dover sole,

The sounds, strong beer. 'Our Hugues
Should get a haircut.' His hair smelling
Of whiskey, his voice like a coffin,
His bum stuck to the ground.

There is the sea, where he smirks and
Mumbles hello to friends. So close at times
At night. The past is small change of
Dried dreams and drinks. Death a strange

Tumbler surrounded by pernicious pleasures:
Let the words come to me. Let the
Words that will no more be written
Come to me. I'll wait.

You Hugues, you Paul, you Herman, you Eddy,
Word-impostors, brothers in stone script.
Seasoned womanisers steeped in
Everlasting bathos. Let those words come

To me like sighs from the grave, hellish burns,
Love bites, French kisses, nicotine stains.
I get the bottle from the fridge, get out the glass
And celebrate. Tasting oysters, brine from the past.

For poet and painter Paul Snoek

– a belated in memoriam –

No, I won't forget you in these
Bleak November days, in these stormy

Leaf falls, the emptiness of dark grey
Skies and your despair that stormed

And seeped autumnally. I think of you.
You die every year with your bald bleeding

Head on the dashboard and I
Don't know what music suits you best.

Raise a jug of water over your bald head
And do not hesitate to drink of it.

It'll taste thin and give a thirst,
For hair is memory, a pure

Tasting of fresh dates, of
Savoury times, oysters banks

Filled with juicy coolness, vinaigrette
On mussels and always that dry

White wine that you punished
Heavily, grinning broadly.

Your soul was in your eyes and every word
A wheat sheaf, braille without a brush.

The air smelled of blue and your hand
Was a pirate flag, unforgiving.

Deserts sprinkled with water, the
Sand wetted and Death a grey

Shrimp on damp, green lettuce. Napkin
Signed for Aunt Euphoria. Fame is

What's left to us, 'for truth is a
Load of balls that is beyond you.'

Raise your head, speak in innocence
And deny the concrete. Hunter burning

His powder in gloom. Champagne master
Of dry tears. Forgotten now the

Scar of Spermalie, the women
Who cried in your distant, deserted

Arms. The watches ticking in the
Inside pockets of your journeys.

Charlatan of the Painted Sorrow!
Friend from an oh-so distant past.

Nocturnes

Do the tones of your voice linger or
Is it a memory, murmur of the sea?
A mixture of shells on wet sand,
Hesitant foam, razor shell.

The evening's slow approach to dusk,
Your hand on dune and reed. Let
This touch be slow and tender, the word
Brush your lips without hurt.

Glass beads yes, but could I be
The victim of the night, lover
Strangled in hemp, and you are
Not sure. You rise, listen to the

Field piano, the sounds of curly
Lettuce, half-hearted tones of 'please
Remember' and the greenish evanescence
That used to sparkle, and was gone.

How do fingers swerve across a piano?
Or do they roam the keys in vain?
You must drip water in your night head
And atomise your nose to point each letter

To its place and then lean gently
Back in your rocking chair that
No longer touches the dawn. Night-
Urns in the rising sun, golden – ashes – soft.

I hide in the crook of the iron
Hoe and do not yield to the head-
Hunters. Would not, throat slashed, be
Displayed for sale in fish markets on

Marble slabs, but tinkle like Beluga and
Roll on your tongue, fish roe, caviar.
Night song of the chromosomes, the dance
Of innocents, performed in up-tempo.

How to forget such a slow waltz.
Buy the music box of memory and
Play that song again and again. See how
You dance, kiss, turn and linger. See the

Snow fall and shiver at the red drops
Erasing the frostwork of past winters,
Rocking the notes inside yourself,
Hiding your tears in the crook of your arm.

A farewell; you tumble into the arms of the
Blind pianist, who scrapes the sediment out of
Your ears. Squandering notes, squashing black
On white. Waving his stick to scratch and slash.

As if he's defying furious looks with his
Nails rasping on the browned ivories of a
Jangling instrument. Parting is forever
Fumbling in a flat and toneless waste.

The mother is chiselled in a head
Filled with throbbing. Ceaseless
Throbbing. The mother is a
Splitting-wedge that throbs and

Talks bosh, till death implores
Her: Mother dear do stop chiselling,
Do stop throbbing, do stop splitting,
For what happened to your dear ones?

How wind can blow through leaf,
Sounds be released from the hand
Of the poet who imagines a voice,
Writes words for it and

Lets these words settle in a
Nocturnal glass that pearls and foams.
Death is a black square. Death
Is a red cloud in speechless ice.

Come, let us travel once more to
That country and tune our lips
To each other, looking for the
Right wines, now we've still got time

To wipe away, to drench the song
Of our senses and our wrinkles.
Autumn rules. The fall of the leaves.
Come, there is no danger, come.

Hesitant words, hesitant notes until
Death follows. Exasperatingly slow
Silence is murdered by soft
Finger music. She hides her cooing

In monotonous velvet and stammers
Piano. On a new southern day,
In the poet's house the cockerel
Crows, so full of himself.

The unending song / Canto Ostinato

The poet, squatting down, is the supplier
Of words without notes. Tapping away
On ivory keys. Rereading love and letters on
White paper. The word is a stranger,
Looking for shelter. Wanting just another
Word with her. The years. Yes, the years
Flowing shamelessly like the changing tides

Through Zeeland. Dreamless Zeeland
When I am not there. Dreamed Zeeland
When I walk along the beach.
Tones of seething notes, high tide notes.
Wreck master haunted by whisperings and
Drowned Germans. If only they had not,
If only they had not. And always the water.

I'd much rather opt out said the
Boy and he belched and spat out the
Eucharist, the white notes of the past.
And always that unending song that will
Go on, even with severed fingers. No
More obligations. The wide beach,
Orderly ribbed, arch supports of sand.
Harsh light and taste of briny death.

I must talk with you among the
Marram in the brackish dunes and
How old we were then and how we looked
Out for each other and the hollow was a
Chair in which we sat, sheltered
From every season. Sheltered from
The rain, the wind, the tidings. When
The west wind got up, increased.

Reduced hearing to stammering. One
Didn't know who spoke a word, a word
Composition of leaf or leaves. Deaf-ear.
Rush-wind, swelling to a summer storm.
Where we had looked one another so
Deeply into the eyes. We, sitting there
In that hollow, the wind blowing inland.
We, like life-boats hacked from salt.

Crystal sparkle behind marram grass.
A sea mirage of distant ships,
Water of the Scheldt lingering on the
Horizon, just on the turn. Flood-
Words, flood-drenched language. There is
Comfort dry as buckthorn. There's prickling
On a monochrome day in November.

Lifeless sails, plumes of smoke passing.
Container ships, a cardboard setting in a
Silence full of pop songs and nostalgic cards.
No, nothing has happened. Let's talk it over
You and I, a spring tide later, where water
Turns, falls silent in the foaming sand. Shells
Crack, the razor shell breaks in my hand.

It is one of those nights

It is one of those nights when tractors
Growl in the backyard. Snap at my ear drums
Like hoarse hounds. It is one of those
Nights when endless snarling raises
A fist against the starless sky, mourning

Is proclaimed in vanished streets. It is
One of those nights when names keep
Spinning in the holes of a shrinking
Memory. Names like old clothes in gunny
Bags, even names dreamt up. It is

One of those nights when faces fade in
Coffins, are burnt in ovens, moulder
In earth. And it is one of those nights when
I rake up speech, gather words, grouse within
Myself, and the blinds come crashing down.

It is one of those nights when my father sits
Down unannounced at the table and I pour
Out a drink, and he empties his first glass
Thirstily, signals for another, loosens
His tie and lights a cigarette. From an

Inside pocket he produces faded photos, points
At himself and nods. I recognize the man
From the past, so close to myself that I shrug
Death from my shoulders, feeling shy again.
It is one of those nights when his voice reaches

Out for sound and son. Each glass a step
To bring us closer, cigarettes hiding shyness.
And when the bottle is empty, cigarettes finished,
He retires into his night, and I am left behind,
While daylight slowly taunts my eyes.

It is one of those nights that envelop me
Like a wet duffel coat weighting me down,
In which I stagger on after a downpour,
Reach my home. It is one of those nights
When memory scrapes like a sharp knife

And flakes whirl down. Silence as
Deep as a snowfall, which miraculously
Touches the dead. It is one of those nights
When your presence reaches out and nestles
Close to me. I kiss you with pursed lips.

Former tenderness reasserts itself. It is
One of those nights when rain drips on the
Floor of remembrance, and drips, and your
Head lies still on your drenched pillow
And you can only cry and cry.

Consul

Bathing in sweat, armpits like rivers,
He drags his worn-out shoes to the
Pub. Sweat staining the brim of his
Straw hat. The consul exudes thirst.

And the thirsty Consul must drink.
To preserve honour in defeat,
Freeze the dance of death, exorcise
His loved ones the Consul

Orders his drinks, and drinks in
God-awful bars, where the stench of
Urine rises from the floorboards. Cackling

Of stray chickens grates on
His eardrums. The Consul rests his
Head on the bar, opens his mouth.

Lovingly he fills his thirsty organs,
Gulps down grief by the mouthful and
Wishes to die in spasms of alcohol. The
Volcano spews down its contempt.

That night he drops down like a bag of
Potatoes in a street in Cuernavaca.
That night, his hangover gone like dust,
The daily ritual is resumed and the Consul

Re-enters El Farolito, hidden under his
Panama. He seems to have forgotten the
Stones. She, the wound that chafes,

Clings to the gossamer the late night
Laces round him, and he vents his gall of
Fear and love on the bare slabs.

Thus he wakes up in the blazing sun.
Donkeys passing by. Smirking people.
The Consul gets to his feet, gropes for
His hat and covers his balding head.

Tastes the sand between his teeth,
Staggers and gnashes in anger.
His thirsty tongue like leather and
His uvula a burnt-out attic of

Smoked fish. There's nothing but blind
Thirst in this zenith. In his head the
Letter tasting like dry plaque.

He staggers forward and thinks of her
Welcome. He needs to be sober, recall
A past, embraces and lips.

The Consul writes carefully and hesitates
On the mescal-drenched paper, letters
Fade in the damp, occasionally the ink
Remains legible, words stare up at him.

He loses track and mumbles her name.
He must not lose his speech. She is the
Interference in his brain. She who comes
Like the Holy Mother with breasts full of roses,

She who comes like mercy for his words, who
Must comfort the Consul, smother the volcano
In his head, quench the magma of his thirst.

She dies here and now. The Consul hurls
Emptied bottles at chimaeras and sobs for her
Death, though she's not due until tomorrow.

I will call her Dolores, my Mother of
Sorrows, who quenches, anoints and soothes
Wounds and I will never have another drop
Under her wakeful eye and will taste the

Cool of the evening, as before near the lake
In Canada. She will present her lips and
I will kiss them. Taste her cool breath
Soberly. All shall be well, if only

She will come and I shall embrace her.
God, he thinks, is mescal, stopping every
Questioning word. She is my illusion,

Who will bend over me and kiss the sand
From my lips. Dogs are barking in
Cuernavaca. The cock in the Consul crows.

Notes

Some of these poems were translated by Peter Nijmeijer ('Dream in time of the hunted', 'Picture postcard', 'Where the blue ends', 'The thirst of ports', 'Evening fall'), Peter Galinski ('Asparagus, asparagus') and Claire Nicolas White ('Seascapes').

'Brewhouse farm' is for painter Theo Kuijpers.

'Yonder, to Ghent' Dedicated to my grandfather Polydorus de Valkenaere from Ghent.

'Walker' In memory of the poet Hans Berghuis.

'Studio' In memory of the painter Pieter Defesche.

'The wine is a mocker' and 'Going Down Slow' In memory of the painter Pierre van Soest.

'Across the fields' is for Seamus Heaney, walking together after a visit to Thoor Ballylee, Gort, Co. Galway.

'Glass' In memory of the publisher Jo Peters.

'Slow approach' is for my brother R.

'For the love of women' Reminiscences of four Flemish poets, who died too soon:
Hugues C. Pernath (1931-1975), Paul Snoek (1933-1981),
Herman de Coninck (1944-1997), Eddy van Vliet (1942-2002).

'Nocturnes' Inspired by the nocturnes of the Irish composer John Field (1782-1837). This cycle of poems was published in May 2006 in a limited edition of 50 copies by the Bonnefant Press of Banholt (Netherlands).

'The Unending Song / Canto Ostinato' Composed by Simeon ter Holt and performed by Kees Wierenga and Polo de Haas, pianists. Published in October 2007 in a limited edition of 50 copies by the Bonnefant Press of Banholt (Netherlands) with two hand-coloured etchings by the painter Jörg Remé.

'Consul', Cuernavaca October 2009, 2nd version 18 November 2009. Bonnefant Press, Christmas 2009.

 **EYEWEAR** PUBLISHING

EYEWEAR POETS

MORGAN HARLOW MIDWEST RITUAL BURNING
KATE NOAKES CAPE TOWN
RICHARD LAMBERT NIGHT JOURNEY
SIMON JARVIS EIGHTEEN POEMS
ELSPETH SMITH DANGEROUS CAKES
CALEB KLACES BOTTLED AIR
GEORGE ELLIOTT CLARKE ILLICIT SONNETS
HANS VAN DE WAARSENBURG THE PAST IS NEVER DEAD
DAVID SHOOK OUR OBSIDIAN TONGUES